FOOD TRUCK BUSINESS HANDBOOK FOR BEGINNERS AND PROFESSIONALS

Step by step on how to start and still finish

A Basic Strategic Framework for Establishing and Sustaining a Prosperous Mobile Food Business

FLETCHER M COOK

Copyright ©2024 **FLETCHER M. COOK**

No part of this publication may be reproduced, distributed, or transmitted in any form or by any means, including photocopying, recording, or other electronic or mechanical methods, without the prior written permission of the publisher, except in the case of brief quotations embodied in critical reviews and certain other noncommercial uses permitted by copyright law. For permission requests, write to the publisher.

This is a tactic that might perhaps enable you to make a significant influence.

Greetings, distinguished readers,

We appreciate your choice of the **"FOOD TRUCK BUSINESS HANDBOOK"** I am delighted to provide you with this extensive resource that seeks to alleviate the difficulties associated with food safety management. The purpose of this book is to provide both inexperienced and experienced food service managers with the necessary information and skills to ensure food safety, maintain rigorous standards, and enhance their professional growth. Additionally, it offers advantageous career guidance.

I appreciate your views. If you see this book to be beneficial, enlightening, or life-changing, I respectfully ask that you spare a minute to write a good review. Your support not only enhances the discoverability of our site but also fosters its continuous expansion and provision of top-notch content.

I appreciate your valuable time, trust, and assistance. Let's work together to make dining for everyone safer and healthier.

Regards,

TABLE OF CONTENTS

FOOD TRUCK BUSINESS

Food industry overview

EATING OUT AND RESTAURANTS BENEFITS

CHAPTER 1: RESEARCH AND PLANNING

    Define your target audience.

    how owners of food trucks and restaurants target their audience

    Developing the Concept

CHAPTER 2: LEGAL REGULATIONS REQUIREMENT

    BUSINESS LICENSING AND REGISTRATION

    Typical licenses and permits

    Rules in health and safety

    LICENSE AND CHECKS

    Typical areas of emphasis for inspections

CHAPTER 3: SETUP OF BUSINESS

    SELECTING A SITE

    Supply and equipment

        Provisions for a mobile food truck kitchen

    MENU UPDATES

        key challenges with food truck menu design

challenges in producing menus for restaurants

Chapter 4: Planning and Finances

IDENTITY AND BUDGETING

problems for food truck and restaurant businesses

FINANCIAL OPTIONS

PRICES STRATEGY

Chapter 5: Promotion and Marketing

IDENTITY AND BRAND

MARKING SOCIAL MEDIA

OCCASIONS AND PARTNERSHIPS

CHAPTER 6 OPERATING MANAGEMENT

STAFFING AND TRAINING

RESERVE MANAGEMENT

SATISFACTION OF CUSTOMERS

Difficulties with Regulation and Compliance

Challenges in Operations

Space Restraints:

Inventory Control

The Reliability of Equipment

Monetary Troubles

2. Variations Seasonal

Issues with Competition and Marketing

1. Establishing a clients
2. Position and Movement

Challenges with Staffing

1. Staff Hiring and Retention
2. Staff Attrition

Challenges with Technology

1. POS (Point of Sale) Systems
2. Internet Presence:

Difficulties in Customer Service

1. Expectations from Customers:
2. Resolving Grievances:

Innovation and Flexibility

1. Staying Current with Trends:
2. Getting Used to Shifting Markets

Chapter 7: Expanding and Developing

GROWING YOUR ENTERTAINMENT

EXTENSION AND PROMOTIONS

PARTNERSHIP OPPORTUNITIES

Chapter 8: Understanding the Need for Scaling

The Art of Strategic Planning

1. Research on the market and feasibility study
2. Budgeting

3. Model of Business

Operational Growth

   1. Place Strategy

   2. Menu Enhancement

   3. Employees and Education:

   4. Technological Coordination

Promoting and Developing Brands

   1. Brand Coherence

2. Digital Advertising

   3. Interaction with the Community

Taking Care of Growth

   1. Control of Quality

   2. Management of Finances

   3. Scalability

Assessment of Achievement

   1. Important Performance Measures (KPIs)

   2. Ongoing Enhancement:

Chapter 9: technology and innovation

POS (Point of Sale) Systems

   Portable Point of Sale Systems

2. Making Contactless Payments:

Management of Inventory

   1. Automated Inventory Management:

   2.Chain of Supply Integration

Ordering and Delivery Online

   1.Smartphone Apps and Web Pages

   2.Services Provided by a Third Party

Client Relationship Administration (CRM)

   1.Software for CRM

   2.Loyalty Initiatives

Social Media and Marketing

   1.Social Media Site

   2.Partnerships with Influencers

Information Analytics

   1.Analysis of sales data

   2.Analysis of client feedback

Safe Food Handling and Preparation

   1.Intelligent Kitchen Appliances

   2.Monitoring Food Safety

Efficiency in Operations

   1.Route Optimization Program

   2.Instruments for Staff Scheduling

Eco-Friendly and Sustainable Methodologies

   1.Environmentally Sustainable Packaging

   2.Energy-Consumptive Equipment

Creative Menu and Service Concepts

1. Novel Menu Items:

2. Adjustable Purchases

conclusion

SUMMARY KEY POINTS

1. Overview of the Food business
2. The benefits of food trucks and restaurants
3. business registration and licensing
4. Health and Safety Regulations
5. Permissions and Inspection: Obtaining
6. Selecting a Location
7. Equipment and Supplies
8. Menu Development
9. Budgeting and Identity
10. Staffing and Training
11. Inventory management
12. Customer service
13. Diversification and options
14. Opportunities for Franchising

FUTURE PLAN

FOOD INDUSTRY OVERVIEW

The food industry is a complicated and dynamic area that involves many facets of food transportation, manufacture, and consumption. It is crucial to the global economy because it meets the primordial human desire for eating while showing regional uniqueness and culinary ingenuity. The food business encompasses various industries, including agricultural and food service enterprises, which together produce food for millions of people worldwide.

The basic purpose of the food company is to utilize manufacturing and processing to transform raw agricultural resources into consumable commodities. This comprises livestock and poultry as well as crops like fruits, vegetables, and grains. The techniques employed in agriculture vary widely among locations and are determined by elements such as soil type, climate, and technological progress. The food production sector has experienced a revolution owing to the introduction of sustainable agricultural technologies and organic farming, which has boosted awareness of ethical sourcing and environmental responsibility.

After being collected, raw crops are processed using a variety of procedures to generate final food products. Maintaining product safety and quality involves washing, sorting, packaging, and preservation methods. Food processing facilities occur in different forms and sizes, from modest companies to vast industrial complexes. They all specialize in distinct product categories, like packaged snacks, frozen entrees, or canned products. Innovations in food processing operations, such as the introduction of innovative preservation methods, fortification tactics, and alternative ingredients, have been enabled by improvements in food science and technology.

In the food sector, distribution is vital to delivering items to clients on time and safely. This refers to a network of distributors, wholesalers, retailers, and suppliers who work together to distribute and store food goods from production locations to ultimate consumers. Food distribution depends largely on logistics and supply chain management, with issues like transportation costs, storage capacity, and inventory control impacting the system's performance. Online grocery shops and e-commerce have become key actors in the food distribution market in recent years, providing consumers with simple replacements for traditional brick-and-mortar enterprises.

Numerous factors, such as dietary choices, lifestyle decisions, and cultural standards, determine how much food individuals consume. Because of this, a broad variety of enterprises are included in the food industry, from fast-food franchises to fine dining places to street vendors and food trucks. The food service company's components each offer a range of dining experiences, price points, and cuisines to cater to diverse consumer demographics and interests. Furthermore, consumer demand for better, more sustainable food options has been spurred by dietary trends and health concerns. As a consequence, plant-based diets, organic foods, and locally produced commodities have gained in favor.

There are issues and disputes in the food business. Recent years have witnessed a growth in interest in themes like labor standards, food safety, and sustainability, which has driven industry players to implement tougher rules and moral requirements. The food supply chain has also evolved as a consequence of globalization and trade agreements, which have fostered the spread of food commodities throughout the world but have also given rise to worries about cultural homogeneity and food sovereignty.

EATING OUT AND RESTAURANTS BENEFITS

Both food trucks and restaurants are key aspects of the food service sector, giving clients varied experiences and benefits. While restaurants offer a typical dining setting in a fixed place, food trucks give flexibility and mobility while serving a broad variety of preferences. Both techniques have benefits in that they appeal to a range of demographics and gourmet trends.

The mobility and agility of food trucks make them unique and allow them to reach a broad spectrum of consumers in several settings. This versatility is especially advantageous in heavily populated urban regions where food trucks may lure customers by taking advantage of festivals, events, and well-known landmarks. Food trucks have greater earning potential as they may react to fluctuating market conditions and customer demand than typical restaurants bound to a specific region.

Compared to brick-and-mortar enterprises, food trucks offer reduced starting and operating expenses, which is one of their key benefits. Food truck operators may start their enterprises with relatively modest expenditures as they don't need pricey real estate or inventive interior design, which makes it an enticing alternative for ambitious company owners. Food trucks also have reduced overhead expenses, which means they require fewer personnel and utilities, which enhances profit margins and flexibility in the budget. Additionally, food trucks give a venue for culinary creativity and innovation by allowing chefs to display their unique dishes and innovative concepts to a big audience. Eating from a food truck encourages a spirit of community and engagement between chefs and consumers, providing for an exceptional eating experience that extends beyond the meal itself. A number of food trucks cater to food aficionados and brave consumers who are in quest of unique tastes and culinary experiences by specializing in specialist cuisines or unconventional fusion dishes. However, restaurants offer a more normal dining experience, complete with a defined location, decor, and amenities. Due to the fact that clients have emotional relationships to their chosen restaurants, their longevity increases brand loyalty and repeat business. Restaurants offer a fantastic atmosphere for folks to relax and enjoy a meal with friends and family. They also commonly serve as gathering areas for social events, festivities, and business meetings.

Another advantage of restaurants is that they give a larger selection of menu items and eating options to satisfy varied dietary demands and preferences. In contrast to food trucks, which might have a limited amount of capacity for cooking and storing items, restaurants are able to handle wider menus and accommodate to dietary restrictions like gluten-free or vegan alternatives. In order to appeal to a larger customer, restaurants may also offer a range of eating experiences, from fast-casual and informal to fine dining.

In addition, restaurants have the capacity to develop a stronger brand identity and presence in their local communities, improving the local economy and culture. Numerous restaurants establish themselves as local monuments, pulling in both residents and visitors with their distinctive cuisines and ambience. Restaurants may create long-term success and sustainability by establishing a committed client base and generating good word-of-mouth referrals via effective marketing and customer interaction.

CHAPTER 1: RESEARCH AND PLANNING

Market research is a vital technique for food truck and restaurant enterprises to appreciate the dynamics of their target market, find potential and difficulties, and design effective strategies. Organizations may strategically position themselves for growth and profitability by examining demographic challenges, consumer preferences, market trends, and competition.

Here's an overview of the important items food truck and restaurant owners should look at when completing a market analysis:

1. Industry Trends: Staying ahead of the competition and spotting opportunities require an awareness of current industry trends. This encompasses eating habits, nutritional preferences, sustainability, wellness, and technology adoption trends. Businesses may acquire insights into new trends and make necessary modifications to their services and strategy by keeping a watch on industry journals, market research studies, and social media trends.

2. Customer Preferences: The success of food truck and restaurant operations is largely impacted by client preferences. Understanding elements like taste preferences, dietary limitations, price sensitivity, convenience, and lifestyle choices is crucial for understanding client preferences. Organizations may acquire insights into consumer decision-making and alter their items to match customer needs and expectations by conducting surveys, focus groups, and customer feedback analysis.

3. Competitive environment: Determining options for differentiation and appreciating competitors' advantages and drawbacks necessitate a detailed examination of the competitive environment. This entails examining both direct and indirect rivals, such as other food trucks or cafes selling similar dishes, as well as fast-food chains, supermarkets, and meal delivery services. Organizations may evaluate competition pricing, menu items, marketing strategies, and customer evaluations, as well as detect market gaps and utilize this knowledge to guide internal decisions and goals by undertaking competitive research.

4. *Customer's behaviors and preferences:* These are impacted by demographic characteristics, including age, gender, family size, economic status, and cultural background. In order to properly contact and connect with these groups, firms should undertake demographic studies of their target market to determine the primary categories. Then, companies may alter their offerings and marketing tactics appropriately. This could involve concentrating on particular demographic groups with specialized message, menu items, and marketing campaigns that match their interests and way of life.

5. *Location Analysis:* A restaurants or food truck company's performance is heavily determined by its location. Companies should carry out a complete site study to identify critical spots with high foot traffic, visibility, and ease of access. The proximity to residential areas, workplaces, tourist locations, transportation hubs, and competing sites are among the aspects to take into mind. Businesses should also examine infrastructure, parking availability, lease terms, zoning limits, and other considerations to make sure the property they pick will support their long-term development plans and operation's needs.

6. *Economic considerations:* A variety of economic factors impact consumer behavior and purchasing power, including GDP growth, employment rates, levels of disposable income, and spending patterns. In order to predict changes in client demand and adapt their pricing, promotions, and services properly, firms should keep an eye on economic statistics and trends. In uncertain or down turning economic times, companies may need to concentrate on value-added services, cost-cutting initiatives, and targeted marketing efforts to remain competitive and survive.

7. *Regulatory Environment:* The operations and compliance of food truck and restaurant companies are influenced by regulatory concerns such as labor laws, licensing requirements, and health and safety standards. To avoid fines, penalties, and harm to their reputation, firms should remain up to speed on regulatory changes and maintain compliance with all applicable laws and regulations. This can entail staying current of industry best practices, implementing food safety policies, getting the required licenses and approvals, and engaging closely with regulatory organizations.

DEFINE YOUR TARGET AUDIENCE.

For food truck and restaurant enterprises to adapt their products, marketing methods, and customer experiences to fit the demands and preferences of their most essential customers, defining the target demographic is a key first step. Businesses may effectively attract, engage, and retain customers by knowing the behavioral, psychographic, and demographic components of their target market. This leads to long-term success and prosperity.

HOW OWNERS OF FOOD TRUCKS AND RESTAURANTS TARGET THEIR AUDIENCE

Demographic information: Information on age, gender, family size, income, education, and employment could give crucial facts about the makeup of the target audience. To identify crucial market segments, such as young professionals, families with children, college students, or the elderly, firms should evaluate demographic data. Organizations may better adjust their menu choices, pricing, portion sizes, and advertising strategies to appeal to a range of customer populations by having a good awareness of demographic aspects.

Psychographic profiles: In-depth insight of the motives and inclinations of the target audience may be achieved by evaluating psychographic features including lifestyle, values, interests, attitudes, and personality traits. Businesses may employ focus groups, surveys, or interviews to acquire insight into the beliefs, interests, and lifestyle choices of their target audience in order to construct psychographic profiles of them. For instance, a food truck catering to health-conscious consumers might focus on delivering organic, plant-based menu selections that meet their dietary requirements and beliefs.

Behavioral Patterns: Businesses may acquire insight into how customers engage with their products and services by examining behavioral components such as eating habits, purchasing patterns, consumption patterns, and loyalty tendencies. Companies may segment their audience according to variables like frequency of visits, average spend per transaction, or willingness to try new menu items by evaluating transaction data, customer feedback, and engagement indicators. Businesses may change their promotional offers, loyalty schemes, and marketing language to encourage desired behaviors and boost client retention by recognizing patterns in customer behavior.

Location-Based Insights: These insights give substantial data on the target audience's concentration and geographic dispersion. Companies may employ customer data analysis, demographic mapping tools, or geographic information systems (GIS) software to find target areas, zip codes, or regions with high levels of disposable income, foot traffic, or population density. Businesses may enhance their site selection, marketing techniques, and operational procedures to more effectively reach and connect with their target audience by concentrating on particular geographic regions.

Competitive Analysis: Examining competitors' target markets may reveal vital information about customer preferences, market segmentation, and unmet needs in the industry. Companies should undertake competition analysis to identify important competitors, analyze their benefits and weaknesses, and investigate their clientele and marketing methods. Businesses may uncover possibilities for distinction, innovation, and market penetration to pull customers away from competitors and increase market share by establishing the target audience of their rivals.

Customer input & Surveys: Businesses may acquire firsthand information of the preferences, expectations, and levels of satisfaction of their target audience by employing surveys, comment cards, or online reviews to get input from their consumers. Customers' views should be constantly obtained by firms in order to grasp their demands, handle any difficulties or concerns, and find opportunities for improvement. Businesses may create closer ties with their target audience and encourage advocacy and loyalty by paying attention to customer input and implementing it into decision-making processes.

Developing the Concept

For food truck and restaurant operations to build their own identity, menu selections, customer experience, and brand positioning, concept creation is a vital stage. Firms may establish a compelling value proposition that attracts customers and supports long-term success by carefully crafting a concept that appeals to their target audience and sets them apart from rivals.

This is a thorough examination of the important phases in the idea-generating process for food truck and restaurant businesses:

Market research: Conducting in-depth market research is the initial step in formulating a concept. This is done to examine consumer trends, appreciate the competitive landscape, and identify the necessity for varied cuisines and dining experiences. To uncover market gaps and potential for differentiation, organizations should investigate the competitors, visit their websites, and interact with prospective customers.

2. Determine Target Audience: Tailoring the concept to the target audience's needs and preferences demands an awareness of their demographic, psychographic, and behavioral features. Companies should undertake a market segmentation analysis to discover important client categories, including families, young professionals, or health-conscious customers, and then build a concept that appeals to their specific interests in food, entertainment, and lifestyle.

3. *Concept Ideation:* This process encompasses producing concepts and ideas for the core idea, menu items, venue, and patron experience of the food truck or restaurant. Companies should analyze variables including the style of cuisine, the cooking method, the eating atmosphere (such as fine dining, fast-casual, or street food), and any unique selling qualities that make the idea stand out from the competition and appeal to the target market.

4. *Menu Development:* Establishing the major offerings and culinary character of a restaurant is a critical aspect of concept formation. In order to accommodate to a broad range of tastes and preferences, companies should establish a menu that represents the concept's theme, showcases distinctive dishes, and offers a variety of flavors, textures, and dietary alternatives. In order to maximize income, menu development may entail undertaking recipe testing, finding quality ingredients, and determining competitive pricing for menu items.

5. *Brand Identity:* Developing a compelling and memorable brand identity is vital to generating an idea that appeals to people. Companies should establish their visual identity elements—such as their logo, color scheme, and typography—that express the heart of their concept and set them apart from competition. Maintaining a consistent brand identity throughout all touchpoints—signs, packaging, clothes, and digital platforms—helps promote brand awareness and loyalty while also confirming the concept's identity.

6. *Customer Experience Design:* Creating an outstanding customer experience is vital to attracting in new business, maintaining current customers, and creating favorable word-of-mouth referrals. Companies have to examine each step of the client journey, beginning from the moment at which consumers first come across the concept and finishing with the actual dining experience. This covers components that contribute to the overall atmosphere and image of the idea, such as mood, design, lighting, music, and staff interactions.

7. Operational challenges: To assure the concept's practicality and scalability, operational difficulties such as supply chain management, workflow design, human needs, and equipment requirements must be addressed. Companies should analyze their infrastructure and operational capacity to determine whether the proposal can be executed and to uncover any bottlenecks or hurdles that may need to be resolved.

8. Testing and Iteration: After an idea is formed, organizations should test and iterate the concept to enhance and alter its components in response to feedback from stakeholders and customers. Before publicly releasing the concept to the public, this may involve soft launches, pilot programs, or pop-up events to measure customer response, collect comments, and make modifications to the idea.

9. Marketing and Promotion: Lastly, in order to communicate the concept to the desired audience and generate anticipation for the launch, organizations should establish a complete marketing and promotion strategy. This can involve employing influencer connections, social media, local advertising, and neighborhood events to develop buzz and drive foot traffic to the food truck or restaurant.

CHAPTER 2: LEGAL REGULATIONS REQUIREMENT

BUSINESS LICENSING AND REGISTRATION

In order to form a valid and legal corporate organization, company registration and licensing are needed. Obtaining the requisite authorizations, permits, and certifications from local, state, and federal authorities in order to legitimately conduct business within a specific jurisdiction is one of these steps. Adherence to registration and licensing criteria is crucial for ensuring legal compliance, preserving intellectual property, and having access to critical services and resources, even if the particular requirements may change dependent on the sort of organization and area. Selecting the suitable legal structure for the organization, such as a corporation, limited liability company (LLC), partnership, or sole proprietorship, is the first step in the business registration process. Regarding responsibility, taxes, and operational flexibility, each legal structure has benefits and drawbacks, so it's vital to thoroughly analyze your choices and, if needed, contact legal and financial specialists.

The next step is to register the business with the necessary government institutions after settling on the legal structure. In most situations, this comprises paying any relevant fees and submitting the appropriate papers to the state or municipal company registration office. It might be important to submit facts about the firm, such its name, location, ownership structure, and projected activities, during the registration process. Organizations may occasionally require an Internal Revenue Service (IRS) federal employment identification number (EIN) in order to submit taxes.

Most firms require extra licenses and permissions in addition to company registration in order to perform legally in a given industry or location. These licenses and approvals, which may be awarded by national, state, or local government bodies, are aimed to assure conformity to zoning, health, and safety rules, among other factors.

Typical Licenses and Permits

1. Business License: Most companies require a general license in order to operate within a given county or municipal jurisdiction. Typically, the application procedure comprises paying a registration cost and supplying basic corporation information.

2. Professional License: In order to perform legitimately, numerous professions, including medical, law, accountancy, and contracts, may require to have specialized licenses or certifications. These licenses may be gained by passing tests or completing specified criteria for education and job experience. State licensing bodies or professional groups commonly give these licenses.

3. Health Permit: In order to guarantee that cleanliness and safety rules are followed, enterprises that offer food service, accommodation, or healthcare may need to secure health permits. Local health organizations typically grant health permits, which may require for site inspections of the enterprise.

4. Zoning Permit: In order to assure compliance with local land use restrictions, companies that operate out of physical places, such as restaurants, retail stores, or manufacturing facilities, may need to secure zoning permits. Problems with building sizes, parking limitations, signs, and noise levels are all regulated by zoning approvals.

5. Alcohol License: State or local alcohol control boards may demand alcohol licenses or permits for facilities that sell or distribute alcoholic beverages, including restaurants, bars, and liquor stores. These licenses, which may impose age limits and background checks, control the distribution, sale, and consumption of alcoholic beverages.

The licenses and permits that the firm requires to function may be stopped or terminated, and there may be penalties and other legal implications if the licenses and approvals are not secured. Furthermore, organizations who operate without the proper legal authorization face the danger of major liability difficulties as well as a reduction in client trust.

RULES IN HEALTH AND SAFETY

Government agencies implement health and safety standards to safeguard the public, customers, and workers in a range of industries and work situations. By providing safe working conditions, enforcing proper cleanliness standards, and lowering health hazards, these measures seek to decrease accidents, injuries, and infections. For organizations of all sizes and sectors to safeguard people and retain organizational integrity, adherence to health and safety requirements is vital.

Workplace safety is one of the key concerns addressed by health and safety legislation. It is the obligation of companies to ensure a safe and healthy work environment for their workers. This comprises identifying and minimizing hazards, delivering proper safety training and personal protective equipment (PPE), and carrying out emergency measures. Common safety laws for the workplace include topics like electrical safety, mechanical safety, handling hazardous materials, and fire prevention.

Standards for health and safety encompass not only workplace safety but also public health problems relating to food safety and hygiene.

Rigid hygiene requirements apply to enterprises that handle, prepare, and serve food in order to prevent contamination and foodborne diseases. These rules frequently include suggestions for appropriate handling, preparation, serving, and storage of food as well as periodic compliance assessments by health authorities.

Regulations linked to health and safety help preserve the environment, particularly in industries that handle or create dangerous products or pollutants. In order to limit their influence on the environment and nearby communities, companies are expected to conform to regulations relating to waste management, pollution control, and environmental sustainability. This can involve establishing plans for minimizing pollution, conducting recycling activities, and keeping an eye on the environment to verify that rules are being followed.

Furthermore, in the healthcare industry, where patient safety and treatment quality are critical, health and safety laws are highly significant. To ensure the health and wellness of both patients and staff, healthcare facilities are expected to follow stringent norms and procedures for infection control, sterilization, medication delivery, and patient confidentiality. Healthcare workers obtain advice and instructions from regulatory authorities like the Occupational Safety and Health Administration (OSHA) and the Centers for Disease Control and Prevention (CDC) to ensure that health and safety rules are followed.

Health and safety rules are enforced via audits, inspections, and punishments for noncompliance. If remedial action isn't done to address the difficulties, firms that are determined to violate health and safety standards face fines, citations, legal action, or even closure. Furthermore, non-compliance may result in severe financial losses and punishments from the government, harm a company's image, and lose consumer trust.

LICENSE AND CHECKS

To ensure public health and safety, permits and inspections are crucial components of operating a food company. They assure conformity to health, safety, and sanitary laws. Regulatory obligations for food operations include getting the proper approvals and going through frequent inspections in an attempt to restrict health hazards, halt foodborne diseases, and maintain cleanliness standards throughout the food production and distribution process.

To begin utilizing the permission and inspection procedure, discover the precise permits necessary for the sort of food firm being conducted. These could include specific licenses for things like outdoor dining, food carts on wheels, or the serving of alcoholic drinks, in addition to permissions for the handling, serving, cooking, and storage of food. The particular approvals necessary may alter depending on criteria such as the company's location, the sort of food supplied, and the number of events.

Submitting permit applications to the relevant regulatory bodies—such as licensing boards, environmental health agencies, or municipal health departments—comes next after the essential permits have been identified. Applications for permits frequently contain particular facts about the organization, including the name and location of the business, the ownership structure, the menu selections, the methods used to handle food, and the design of the facility. Organizations may occasionally need to undertake pre-approval inspections in addition to seeking permits.

Following granting of the relevant permits, food outlets are subject to recurring inspections by health department inspectors who check conformity to legislation regulating food safety and sanitary requirements. Planned or unplanned, inspections involve extensive reviews of numerous aspects of the organization, such as food handling protocols, sanitation operations, building maintenance, and personnel hygiene. In order to verify compliance with regulatory requirements, inspectors may check records of staff training, temperature logs, cleaning schedules, and food safety plans during inspections.

TYPICAL AREAS OF EMPHASIS FOR INSPECTIONS

1.Food Storage: To make sure that food is stored at the appropriate temperatures and guarded from contamination, inspectors will examine storage places. This comprises shelf units, freezers, dry storage rooms, and refrigerators.

2. Food Preparation: To minimize cross-contamination and foodborne diseases, inspectors will keep an eye on food preparation methods to assure correct handling, cooking, and storage of food. This includes habits like cleansing your hands, wearing gloves, keeping your utensils clean, and utilizing the proper cooking temperature.

3. *Facility cleanliness:* Inspectors will inspect the facility's cleanliness, including the equipment, surfaces, bathrooms, and areas utilized for food preparation. In order to limit the spread of illnesses and assure food safety, companies are expected to maintain a clean and hygienic atmosphere.

4. *staff Hygiene:* To limit the transfer of infections to food products, inspectors will keep an eye on staff hygiene standards, such as personal grooming, handwashing, and food handling abilities.

5. *Pest control:* To prevent contaminating food and areas used for food storage, inspectors will search for evidence of pests like insects, rodents, or other vermin. They will also analyze how effectively pest control approaches are performing.

Organizations may seek inspection reports following an inspection, which detail any violations or flaws detected during the inspection and the required corrective steps for compliance. Depending on the nature of the violations, companies might face fines, penalties, or closure until remedial action is made. Furthermore, organizations may have to undertake follow-up inspections to ensure conformity to regulatory requirements.

CHAPTER 3: SETUP OF BUSINESS

SELECTING A SITE

In the food sector, site selection is vital since it may considerably affect a business's viability and profitability. A food restaurant's location influences a variety of elements, including foot traffic, competitiveness, demographics, and operational expenses, in addition to visibility and accessibility to customers. Thorough research of local circumstances is important before opening a food truck, restaurant, or catering company in order to exploit potential and prevent hazards.

When picking a site for a restaurant, foot traffic and visibility are two crucial concerns. Busy streets, retail malls, tourist locations, and business districts are examples of high foot traffic regions that give increased exposure and possible customer reach. Companies that are located in places where there is a lot of foot activity are more likely to bring in walk-in customers and benefit from improved exposure and brand awareness. However, rental prices may be greater than in less-frequented places thanks to fierce competition for desirable properties in popular districts.

Another key issue to take into consideration when picking a site for a food business is accessibility. Customers should be able to quickly access the facility by a range of means of transportation, such as vehicles, public transit, bicycles, and foot traffic. Accessible roads, conveniently accessible parking spaces, and accessibility to public transit hubs are vital components in assuring that clients may visit the institution without any hassles. Furthermore, firms positioned in close proximity to comparable institutions or sites of interest, including theaters, shopping complexes, or entertainment venues, might notice an increase in foot traffic and customer crossover.

When deciding whether a place is suited for the food business, demographics have a vital effect. By considering the target market's age, income, family size, cultural background, and lifestyle preferences, firms may be able to select regions with the highest prospects of success. A food truck offering street cuisine may thrive in a crowded metropolitan region with a varied population and a dynamic culinary scene, while a gourmet restaurant may prosper in an affluent neighborhood with sophisticated tastes.

When picking a location for a food firm, competitive research is vital to look at market saturation, locate gaps in the market, and differentiate goods. Businesses wishing to make a difference should examine the present food outlets in the area, taking into consideration elements such as menu items, pricing strategies, customer feedback, and brand positioning in order to appreciate the competitive environment. Businesses may separate themselves from the competition and attract in customers in a crowded market by picking a location with fewer direct competitors or delivering a distinct value proposition.

Any food firm must handle the significant problem of operational expenditures as they have an immediate influence on financial sustainability and profitability. Businesses should carefully assess how rental or lease pricing, utilities, taxes, insurance premiums, and other overhead expenditures fit into the budget and revenue predictions before selecting on a location. While premium sites in popular regions may attract higher rents, companies must measure the possible benefits of greater customer traffic and publicity against the higher operational expenses.

Lastly, before picking a place for a food company, regulatory considerations such as zoning constraints, health and safety requirements, and approvals necessary should be thoroughly reviewed and understood. Before launching for business, organizations must make sure that they are in conformity with all relevant local regulations and receive the required licenses and authorization. A location's practicality and acceptability as a site for a food service may be influenced by aspects like zoning limits, noise rules, signage criteria, and permits for outdoor eating.

SUPPLY AND EQUIPMENT

Food preparation, storage, and service are heavily influenced by equipment and supplies, which are vital to the operations of both food trucks and restaurants. Businesses that operate brick and mortar restaurants or mobile food trucks need to make investments in top-notch supplies and equipment to ensure consistency, efficiency, and safety in food preparation and delivery. To maintain operational excellence and satisfy customer expectations, it is necessary to pick the correct equipment and supplies, ranging from cooking utensils and kitchen appliances to serving ware and packaging materials.

Space is generally at a premium in food trucks, so it's vital to highlight equipment that is both tiny and multipurpose in order to optimize efficiency without compromising functionality.

Provisions for a mobile food truck kitchen

1. Cooking equipment: Griddles, fryers, grills, and convection ovens are a few examples of tiny, energy-efficient cooking equipment that are vital for swiftly and efficiently preparing a broad variety of menu items.

2. *Storage and Refrigeration:* To store food at a reasonable temperature and preserve perishable items, refrigeration systems—like reach-in coolers and freezers—are required. The limited space aboard a food truck may be maximized for storage with the use of space-saving storage alternatives include shelf systems, racks, and storage containers.

3. *Food Preparation Equipment:* Food processors, slicers, mixers, and other equipment assist to maintain consistency in food quality and portion proportions while also expediting prep tasks.

4. *Serving ware and packaging:* For the purpose of presenting food to clients and expediting takeaway orders, disposable serving ware, such as plates, bowls, cutlery, and cups, as well as packaging materials, such as containers, wraps, and bags, are important.

5. *Sanitation and cleaning supplies:* The maintaining of cleanliness and sanitation requirements in the restaurant kitchen and dining rooms needs the use of commercial-grade cleaning products including degreasers, sanitizers, detergents, and disinfectants, along with cleaning instruments like mops, buckets, squeegees, and brushes.

To sustain daily operations and fulfill consumer demand, food trucks and restaurants must also make expenditures in high-quality supplies including ingredients, spices, condiments, sauces, napkins, and disposable packaging. In order to preserve food safety and operational efficiency, companies should also put attention to obtaining equipment and supplies that are long-lasting, easy to maintain, and comply with health and safety laws.

MENU UPDATES

Because it has a direct influence on customer enjoyment, profitability, and brand recognition, menu design is a vital component of operating a food truck or restaurant. It includes thorough planning to take into consideration elements such target market preferences, culinary trends, product availability, pricing strategy, and operational capabilities when establishing a well-designed menu. Businesses that manage brick-and-mortar restaurants or food trucks need to build menus that reflect their distinct offerings, fulfill client preferences, and set them apart from competition.

When it comes to food trucks, limitations like limited area for cooking, equipment limits, and mobility restrictions sometimes impact the design of the menu. Food truck menus are frequently smaller and more focused, providing a limited variety of trademark dishes or specialist items that can be cooked quickly and efficiently in a tiny cooking space. It's vital for food truck operators to stress menu items that are visually beautiful, portable, and suited for the preferences of the target population.

key challenges with food truck menu design

1. diverse foods: Spotting and accentuating outstanding meals or specialist dishes that represent the spirit of the food truck's distinct culinary concept. These goods have to be unique, lasting, and express the character of the brand.

2. Portability: Creating menu items that are easy to consume while traveling and that can be served from the food truck window swiftly and efficiently. cuisine truck menus are typically updated with portable products such wraps, tacos, sandwiches, and snacks that are patterned by street cuisine.

3. Seasonal foods: Adding in-season products and flavors to the menu to preserve offerings that are different, compelling, and in accordance with current culinary trends. Limited-edition items and seasonal discounts could generate curiosity and promote customer involvement.

4. Pricing strategy: Developing a plan that finds a balance between customer value, affordability, and profitability. Menus for food trucks normally feature a variety of pricing to accommodate various budgets while keeping profit margins.

Since restaurants frequently offer a broader range of menu items and dining experiences, menu planning is more complicated and sophisticated in a restaurant environment. To meet a broad variety of interests and circumstances, restaurants may present multi-course menus, daily specials, tasting menus, and prix fixe alternatives. Restaurants may also offer private dining choices, catering, and specifically prepared menus for festivals and special events.

challenges in producing menus for restaurants

1. Menu Variety: Providing a broad assortment of meals, snacks, sides, and desserts to satisfy diverse dietary requirements, tastes, and occasions. To attract a larger consumer base, restaurants may also serve vegetarian, vegan, gluten-free, and allergy-friendly food.

2. *Culinary Innovation:* Displaying innovation and ingenuity in the kitchen via creative flavor combinations, in-season products, and distinctive meals that separate the restaurant from its competition. Chefs may partner with regional suppliers, farmers, and craftsmen to acquire exceptional products and deliver memorable dining experiences.

3. *Beverage Program:* Creating a comprehensive beverage program that enriches the complete dining experience and works well with the food choices. A carefully picked range of wines, craft beers, cocktails, non-alcoholic beverages, and specialty drinks customized to the restaurant's concept and cuisine may be included in this.

4. *Menu engineering:* This is the planned arrangement and layout of the menu for optimal profitability and consumer happiness. This involves pricing menu items correctly to boost sales, employing descriptive language and imagery to entice consumers, and marketing high-margin products.

Menu planning is a continual process that includes constant review, change, and adaptation to changing customer tastes, seasonal items, and culinary trends in both food truck and restaurant settings. In the competitive food service business, food firms may build menus that engage their target market, enhance sales, and nurture customer loyalty by stressing innovation, quality, and customer pleasure.

CHAPTER 4: PLANNING AND FINANCES

IDENTITY AND BUDGETING

Two crucial parts of having a successful food truck or restaurant company are finances and identity. Sustaining and developing the company's finances is secured by proper budgeting, and building a unique brand identity stimulates customer involvement and brand recognition. In the competitive food service sector, entrepreneurs that own brick-and-mortar restaurants or food trucks must put their finances and brand first in order to prosper over the long haul.

For food truck and restaurant enterprises, budgeting is vital to financial management because it helps owners to properly allocate resources, analyze expenses, and make well-informed decisions that will maximize earnings and reduce risks. A complete budget must be prepared by identifying all sources of revenue and expenditure, creating financial goals and targets, and putting effective monitoring and cost management measures into operation.

PROBLEMS FOR FOOD TRUCK AND RESTAURANT BUSINESSES

1. starting expenses: Determining and distributing cash for expenditures involved with purchasing or leasing a vehicle, equipment, permits and licenses, initial inventory, advertising, and legal fees. Starting expenses could vary greatly based on the sort of company, location, and amount of activity.

2. continuing expenditures: Calculating continuing expenses for items like labor, utilities, rent or lease payments, food and beverage pricing, insurance premiums, maintenance and repairs, marketing and advertising costs, and administrative overhead. In order to ensure proper financial forecasting and planning, it is vital to supply cash for both fixed and variable expenditures.

3.Revenue Projection: Estimate revenue properly by taking into consideration elements like target market size, pricing strategy, volume of sales, seasonality, and degree of competition.

Revenue predictions are used as a basis for analyzing firm performance and assessing profitability over time.

4. *Cash Flow Management:* Putting cash flow management strategies into effect to guarantee that there is adequate liquidity to pay bills on schedule and finance ongoing operating expenditures. This can involve maintaining proper financial reserves, keeping an eye on accounts payable and receivable, negotiating the best terms of payment with suppliers, and reducing inventory levels to avoid carrying costs.

5. *Contingency planning:* This entails putting money aside for unanticipated expenses and constructing a safety net to withstand financial downturns or calamities in order to prepare for unplanned expenditures and uncertain economic situations. In the event of unanticipated crises, contingency planning ensures organizational continuity and assists in risk management.

A unique identity is crucial for food truck and restaurant operations to stand out in a cluttered market, attract consumers, and develop brand loyalty in addition to budgeting. Identity is made up of factors like customer experience, narrative, visual identity, and brand positioning, all of which work to build an emotional connection with customers and affect how they view the organization.

crucial parts of building an identity for food truck and restaurant operations

1. Brand positioning: Brand positioning is the process of defining the company's unique value proposition and market positioning in order to set it apart from competition and attract the target market. Brand positioning should correspond with customer requirements and preferences while expressing the company's basic values, purpose, and personality.

2. Visual identity: Using features like typefaces, color schemes, logos, signage, and package design to create a consistent visual brand. A great visual identity leaves a lasting impact on customers and assists in enhancing brand recognition.

3. Storytelling: Using storytelling to develop an emotional connection and feeling of authenticity with customers while delivering the brand's narrative, values, and history. Customers may become more loyal and attached to the brand if the narrative, inspiration, and passion behind it are communicated.

4. *Customer Experience:* Creating excellent experiences for customers by being polite, customizing interactions, and creating moments that go above and beyond expectations. A pleasant customer experience creates word-of-mouth referrals, repeat business, and brand loyalty.

5. *Community Engagement:* Establishing relationships with the community by involvement in events, philanthropic projects, collaborations, and sponsorships. Participating in the community develops goodwill, enhances brand awareness, and builds a committed customer.

Food truck and restaurant enterprises may develop a strong foundation for success and longevity in the competitive food service sector by placing a focus on budgeting and identity creation. Well-executed budgeting promotes financial stability and allows well-informed decision-making; conversely, developing a strong brand assist in company identity, brand recognition, and deeper customer engagement. Budgets and identity work together to assist a firm create its brand, enhance consumer loyalty, and achieve long-term growth and profitability.

FINANCIAL OPTIONS

Establishing a food truck company may be a wonderful undertaking that gives the possibility to present your great cuisine to a large audience and enjoy the liberty and flexibility that come with owning a food truck. Nevertheless, owning a food truck involves a major time, energy, and money investment, just like any other business effort. Getting money is frequently a key first step in making your goal of owning a food truck a reality. In this essay, we will analyze numerous financing possibilities open to budding food truck proprietors.

1. Personal Savings and Assets: Using personal savings or assets is one of the easiest methods to start a food truck company. With this option, you may keep absolute control over your company without worrying about interest rates or payback schedules. On the other side, it might necessitate a substantial initial expense, so cautious planning is important.

2. Loans from Family and Friends: Asking for financial aid from close friends or family members is another typical technique to receive financing. Compared to conventional lenders, this strategy may give more flexible terms and cheaper interest rates, hence it could be advantageous. To prevent complications later on, it's vital to handle these connections with honesty and skill.

3. Small Business Loans: A number of banks and other financial institutions give small business loans, particularly to start-up or growing enterprises. Clear business ideas, excellent credit records, and collateral are frequently needed for these loans. Getting a small company loan allows you access to finance without asking you to give up ownership of your organization, even if it may be more cumbersome than other financing choices.

4. Crowdfunding: Entrepreneurs are increasingly adopting crowdfunding platforms such as Indiegogo, Kickstarter, and GoFundMe to raise money for their ideas. You may gather money from a big number of backers by building an appealing campaign and giving prizes or incentives to supporters. Through crowdfunding, you may gather the required finances to start your food truck idea and evaluate public interest in it.

5. *Grants and competitions:* small companies, especially those in the food sector, may profit from a range of grants and competitions. Grants and contests customized expressly for firms are given by bodies such as local economic development agencies and the Small Business Administration (SBA). These options may give considerable financial aid without the pressure of repayment, but they may involve a competitive application procedure.

6. *Angel Investors and Venture Capitalists:* It would be viable for food truck enterprises with considerable growth potential to seek angel investors or venture capitalists for financing. These people or corporations contribute financing in return for shares or ownership holdings in your company. Although it may be tough, securing finance from venture capitalists or angel investors allows you access to huge quantities of money and experience to build your food truck company.

7. Opportunities for franchising or collaborating: In rare situations, forging a strategic collaboration with another firm or joining hands with an existing food truck franchise may give access to finance and resources. Through franchising, you may take advantage of an existing company's brand recognition and backing, while partnerships may give access to finance, resources, or channels for distribution.

PRICES STRATEGY

In the fast-developing food truck sector, pricing is a vital issue that has the potential to establish or ruin your company. In addition to assuring profitability, selecting the correct rates engages people and builds your food truck's perceived value in the neighborhood. We'll look at a number of pricing strategy concepts in this book that are uniquely geared to the particular dynamics of the food truck industry.

1. Cost analysis: To completely appreciate the expenditures connected with running your food truck, undertake a comprehensive cost evaluation before to developing your pricing strategy. This covers fuel, labor, supplies, permits, maintenance, and other miscellaneous expenditures. You may develop a pricing structure that covers your costs and leaves you with a decent profit margin by precisely predicting your expenses.

2. Competitive Analysis: Examine the pricing methods utilized by your competitors to acquire insight of the dynamics of the market and customer expectations. Examine similar food trucks in your community, taking note of their menu offerings, serving sizes, and pricing points. Being competitive is crucial, but don't restrict yourself to merely decreasing your competitors' expenses. Rather, focus on offering exceptional value propositions and quality that exceed your pricing.

3. Value-Based Pricing: When choosing rates, take into consideration the value your food truck delivers to customers. Perceived value may be impacted by a variety of variables, including the quality of the items, the originality of the menu, customer experience, and convenience. Depending on the perceived value and originality of the meals you offer, you may be able to charge extra for gourmet or artisanal cuisine served from your food truck.

4. Menu Engineering: The pricing strategy you pick is heavily determined by your menu. To enhance sales, employ menu engineering strategies to bring attention to high-profit margin goods, accentuate well-liked meals, and price menu items rationally. To raise average transaction value and maximize profitability, take into consideration combo meals, bundling options, and upselling methods.

5. *Dynamic Pricing:* Adaptability is vital in a business as dynamic and unpredictable as the food truck industry. In order to alter prices according to criteria like demand, seasonality, region, and special events, consider about putting dynamic pricing solutions into place. To take advantage of increased demand, you may, for instance, give discounts during calm periods or boost fees at peak hours or popular events.

6. *Clear Pricing:* Establishing trust with your customers' needs being upfront. To eliminate misconceptions and promote transparency, explicitly mention your prices as well as any additional charges, such as taxes or fees. Steer clear of unplanned or hidden expenditures, as they could drive away clients and weaken their faith in your organization.

7. unique Pricing: To pull in more people, improve sales, and build awareness about your food truck, adopt different pricing tactics. Provide time-limited discounts, loyalty schemes, exclusive deals, or package discounts to promote recurrent business and word-of-mouth referrals. Just exercise care when employing promotional pricing techniques to maintain long-term sustainability and profitability.

8. Feedback and Adaptation: Lastly, maintain a careful watch on your pricing strategy and constantly assess it in light of customer feedback, sales statistics, and industry trends. Keep your choices open to modify as required to preserve your competitive edge and fulfill your target audience's shifting requirements and preferences.

CHAPTER 5: PROMOTION AND MARKETING

IDENTITY AND BRAND

In the fast-paced food truck market, where first impressions count and competition is tough, having a unique brand identity may help your company stand out and attract in customers. The branding of your food truck covers everything from its name, logo, and visual aspects to its values, tone of voice, and overall personality. This article will look at the core elements of branding identification and teach you how to develop a unique and attractive brand for your food truck business.

1. *Identify Your Unique Selling Proposition (USP):* To begin, consider what makes your food truck distinct from the competitors. Your brand identity is generated from your unique selling proposition, which may be anything from your signature dish to your culinary talent, cultural influence, or devotion to sustainability. Your branding efforts will be directed by this

USP, which will also assist in expressing your value proposition to your target market.

2. Choose a Catchy Name: When a potential customer sees your food truck, their attention is generally attracted to its name, so create a favorable impression. Choose a name that is both memorable and easy to say, and that conveys the core of your brand's personality, food, or concept. To make sure your selected name is not already in use and matches with your brand's strategy and values, consider about undertaking market research.

3. Create a Distinctive Logo: Improving brand recognition and leaving a lasting impression demand a visually attractive and memorable logo. Collaborate with a professional graphic designer to develop a logo that represents the soul of your food truck business, integrates the colors and fonts you've picked, and appeals to your target demographic. Your logo should be versatile enough to be utilized on a range of branding materials, such as social media accounts and signage.

4. Create a Consistent Visual Identity: Great branding demands consistency. Create a consistent visual identity that incorporates pictures, typography, color schemes, and design components in addition to your logo. These visual cues need to transmit the proper sentiments, reflect the core of your company, and give a cohesive brand experience across all touchpoints, such as menus, packaging, uniforms, and promotional materials.

5. Develop Your Brand Voice and Messaging: Your food truck business's tone, lexicon, and personality are all determined by your brand voice. Make sure your brand voice corresponds with your target audience and corporate values, regardless of whether you want to be lighter and whimsical, smart and intelligent, or pleasant and easygoing. Create crucial phrasing that conveys your brand's story, communicates your USP, and actually engages shoppers.

MARKING SOCIAL MEDIA

For food truck and restaurant operations, social media marketing has become a crucial tool for customer connection, brand visibility, engagement, and sales growth. As social media platforms like Facebook, Instagram, Twitter, and TikTok grow more extensively utilized, companies have never-before-seen possibilities to sell their products, communicate with customers in real time, and target specialized audiences. In the fast-paced food service industry, firms that operate brick-and-mortar restaurants or mobile food trucks may achieve success by skillfully leveraging social media marketing.

The potential of social media marketing to reach a big audience and generate brand recognition at a very cheap cost is one of the primary benefits for food truck and restaurant enterprises. By developing interesting content, posting mouthwatering food photographs and videos, and connecting with followers, companies may attract in new customers, improve foot traffic, and enhance sales potential. Additionally, social media platforms allow companies specialized advertising alternatives that help them target particular demographics, interests, and geographic locations, enhancing the efficacy of marketing campaigns and maximizing return on investment.

Social media marketing not only reaches a huge audience but also helps food truck and restaurant owners make real relationships with consumers and generate a sense of community around their company. Businesses may develop a dialog with customers, display honesty and transparency, and eventually cultivate trust and loyalty by continuously communicating with their followers, replying to messages and comments, and soliciting feedback and reviews. Social media also gives chances for user-generated content, in which people post their dining experiences, images, and reviews; these contributions act as crucial brand ambassadors and customer testimonials.

The capacity of social media marketing to enhance traffic and profitability via targeted promotions, contests, and unique discounts is another plus for food truck and restaurant enterprises. Social media platforms may be used by companies to publicize impending events or pop-up locations, highlight menu specials, give discounts or coupons, and enhance customer referrals and check-ins. Businesses may push followers to visit their locations, test new menu items, and take advantage of special promotions by generating a sense of urgency and exclusivity. This will enhance foot traffic and income.

OCCASIONS AND PARTNERSHIPS

Food truck and restaurant enterprises may extend their client base, attract in new clients, and enhance their brand recognition within the community by collaborating with events and events. Events and partnerships allow companies the ability to exhibit their goods, connect with customers, and create memorable experiences that drive repeat business and word-of-mouth referrals. Examples of these activities include taking part in food festivals, arranging pop-up events, cooperating with other enterprises, and supporting neighborhood get-togethers. Food truck and restaurant enterprises may separate themselves from competitors, increase awareness, and establish a sense of community around their brand by strategically leveraging events and collaborations.

One typical technique used by food truck and restaurant operators to reach a big audience and exhibit their services in a pleasant and energetic setting is to take part in food festivals, fairs, and events. culinary festivals give companies with a venue to promote new menu items, receive media exposure, and develop relationships with culinary fans and influencers. Businesses who set up booths or food trucks at these events may connect with guests, offer them samples, and build favorable brand impressions that remain long after the event.

Another wonderful tactic utilized by food truck and restaurant entrepreneurs to build excitement and drive consumers to their facilities is to conduct pop-up events. Pop-up events allow companies the ability to test out new ideas, review menu items, and engage with customers in fresh and intriguing ways. Pop-up events, such as themed dinners, guest chef collaborations, or live music performances, build excitement and enthusiasm among consumers, boosting foot traffic and gaining attention from social media platforms.

Through collaborations with other firms, organizations, or personalities, operators of food trucks and restaurants may extend their consumer base and connect with existing networks. partnerships may take many various forms, including social media partnerships, co-branded food items, cross-promotional events, and cooperative initiatives. Organizations may widen their reach, acquire access to shared resources, and build win-win relationships that increase business performance by partnering with partners who have similar values and target audiences.

Food truck and restaurant enterprises may also host their own events and promotions in addition to external events and collaborations in order to engage with customers and enhance sales. Businesses may build excitement and anticipation among customers by giving special prices, live entertainment, or menu items that are unique to them, whether they are conducting a grand opening celebration, anniversary party, or seasonal promotion. Businesses may improve attendance and engagement, leading to increased exposure and revenue, by employing social media, email marketing, and in-store signage to promote events

CHAPTER 6 OPERATING MANAGEMENT

STAFFING AND TRAINING

Since personnel and training have a direct impact on customer enjoyment, service quality, and operational efficiency, they are vital components of operating a successful food truck or restaurant company. Building a talented team that can give consumers with excellent experiences includes recruiting and keeping experts, providing in-depth training, and fostering a healthy work environment. In order to ensure successful operations and continued success in the competitive food service sector, companies, whether operating brick-and-mortar restaurants or food trucks, need to put a heavy focus on staff development and training.

For food truck and restaurant enterprises, the first step in developing a high-performing team is identifying and employing the appropriate individuals. Companies need to write job descriptions that explain tasks, requirements, and expectations for the particular roles and positions—such as chefs, cooks, waiters, bartenders, hosts, and managers—that are necessary to support their operations. In order to attract top talent, recruiting strategies may include posting job adverts on social media, industry networks, online job boards, and local job fairs. Networking with culinary schools, hospitality programs, and industry specialists is another method.

Thorough training is essential after employing staff members to ensure they have the confidence, knowledge, and ability to carry out their jobs and give customers with great service. Aspects of employment activities such as food preparation, POS systems, customer service standards, safety and sanitary laws, and cooperation and communication skills should all be incorporated in training programs. To increase learning and progress, training may be offered via a combination of classroom lectures, practical demonstrations, shadowing of competent individuals, and continual coaching and feedback.

Continuous professional development is vital for staff retention and career growth in food truck and restaurant operations, in addition to initial training. It is advised that organizations offer chances for continual learning, such as workshops, seminars, certifications, and cross-training programs, to allow workers to better their abilities, keep up to speed with industry advances, and grow within the firm. Businesses may empower individuals to succeed in their professions, take on greater responsibility, and contribute to the success of the firm by establishing a culture of learning and development.

Another crucial aspect in building a healthy work environment that stimulates collaboration, morale, and employee engagement is personnel and training. Establishing strong links with workers, fostering frank communication, appreciating and rewarding performance, and giving possibilities for both cooperation and criticism should all be top goals for organizations. Organizations may establish a good and inviting work climate where workers feel valued, motivated, and interested in the company's success by valuing their contributions, hearing what they have to say, and giving chances for growth and improvement.

Furthermore, effective staffing and training methods are crucial to ensure adherence to labor, health, and safety requirements in the food service business. Companies are expected to offer personnel with training on food safety requirements, hygiene norms, limitations on selling alcohol, and workplace safety precautions in order to minimize incidents, injuries, and fines from the government. Businesses may safeguard the health and safety of their workers and customers, keep in compliance with industry rules, and decrease risks to the firm by prioritizing staff training and paying attention to legal requirements.

RESERVE MANAGEMENT

Since inventory management directly influences operational performance, cost control, and customer happiness, it is a vital element of operating a successful food truck or restaurant company. Optimizing inventory levels, reducing waste, keeping a watch on food and drink supplies, and assuring quick replenishment to match customer demand are all part of excellent inventory management. Businesses that operate brick-and-mortar restaurants or food trucks must adopt thorough inventory management methods to generate income and avoid risks in the fast-paced food service business.

Maintaining detailed records of inventory levels in order to reduce stockouts, overstocking, and rotting is one of the key principles of inventory management. For all food and beverage goods, companies must maintain detailed records of inventory counts, consumption rates, and expiration dates in order to assure that they have enough inventory on hand to fulfill customer demand without going overboard. By automating inventory monitoring, creating real-time reporting, and offering insights into inventory performance and trends, inventory management software solutions may make this process simpler.

Establishing inventory levels is critical for food truck and restaurant organizations trying to decrease expenditures and improve income. Organizations may minimize carrying costs, decrease the risk of waste and obsolescence, and enhance cash flow management by specifying par levels, reorder points, and inventory turnover ratios for important components and supplies. Just-in-time inventory management systems may also assist firms minimize their demand for storage space and free up cash for excess inventory, which will enhance corporate operations and free up resources for other departments. Another crucial part of inventory management for food truck and restaurant enterprises is avoiding loss and rotting. To guarantee that older inventory is consumed before new inventory to minimize rotting and expiration, organizations must employ inventory rotation procedures such first-in, first-out (FIFO) and batch cooking. To detect and rectify areas of waste and inefficiency, organizations should also perform physical inventory counts on a regular basis, keep an eye on inventory loss, and apply inventory management strategies include portion control, recipe standardization, and waste monitoring.

For food truck and restaurant enterprises to stay operating and fulfill consumer demand, quick inventory restocking is crucial. To guarantee the timely delivery of fresh, high-quality products and resources, companies need to create outstanding supply chain partnerships with their vendors, distributors, and suppliers. In order to maintain flawless operations and pleased consumers, firms may cut lead times, avoid stockouts, and optimize inventory replenishment processes by predicting demand, keeping an eye on inventory levels, and proactively dealing with suppliers.

To ensure effective operations and compliance with health and safety regulations, organizations must keep and monitor non-food commodities including cleaning supplies, kitchen equipment, and disposable packaging in addition to managing the inventory of food and drinks. Inventory goods must be kept, sorted, and labeled accurately to avoid contamination, loss, and damage while also keeping staff workstations nice and organized.

Additionally, employing technology in food truck and restaurant enterprises to speed up inventory management procedures, enhance accuracy, and raise efficiency is achievable via the use of barcode scanning, RFID tagging, and inventory management software systems. These systems assist firms discover trends, make better buying decisions, and boost overall performance of inventory management by automating inventory monitoring, resolving inventory counts, and delivering reports and analytics.

SATISFACTION OF CUSTOMERS

In the food truck and restaurant businesses, offering good customer service is vital as it enhances client enjoyment, loyalty, and repeat business. Providing exceptional customer service is more than simply preparing wonderful meals; it covers the full contact that customers experience with the firm, from the moment they place their order until they are pleased and walk out. Businesses that manage brick-and-mortar restaurants or food trucks must emphasize offering exceptional customer service in order to stand out from the competition, develop lasting relationships, and give memorable eating experiences. Making consumers feel welcome and warmly accepted is one of the most crucial parts of delivering good customer service in food truck and restaurant enterprises. From the minute visitors arrive, they are made to feel valued and appreciated by a kind smile, a warm greeting, and attentive service that sets the tone for the complete dining experience. To personalize the experience and go above and beyond expectations, staff members should be educated to greet customers straight immediately, call them by name when feasible, and inquire about their dining preferences or any special requests.

Accurately and swiftly collecting and processing orders is a vital aspect of delivering outstanding customer service. Customers expect their orders to be taken swiftly, professionally, and with attention to detail whether they are ordering from a food truck window or a restaurant table. Employees should pay careful attention to what clients ask for, repeat orders back to make sure they are right, and let the kitchen staff know about any specific instructions or dietary restrictions. To ensure a great dining experience, orders should also be made and delivered swiftly while paying attention to quality and appearance. In food truck and restaurant enterprises, giving outstanding customer service demands attentive and responsive communication. Employees needed to be on hand straight away to handle any concerns, give instruction, and manage any difficulties that may emerge while dining. Effective communication establishes strong connections with customers, promotes trust and confidence in the firm, and assures that their needs and expectations are fulfilled or exceeded.

Furthermore, effective customer service in food truck and restaurant operations entails anticipating and exceeding the requirements and expectations of the client. To enhance the dining experience and demonstrate concern and empathy, staff members might be proactive in anticipating the needs of their consumers. This may involve giving complimentary menu items, refilling drinks, or bringing additional condiments or napkins. Making the additional effort to fulfill particular requests, handle difficulties, or amaze and thrill consumers with unforeseen acts or incentives produces a lasting impression and generates word-of-mouth referrals and loyalty.

In food truck and restaurant enterprises, offering exceptional customer service demands a clean, courteous, and attractive atmosphere. Guests expect a clean, well-maintained atmosphere that displays the competence and attention to detail of the institution, whether they are dining at a restaurant or on a food truck. To generate a pleasant impression and enhance the complete eating experience, personnel should frequently clean and disinfect dining rooms, toilets, and kitchen facilities. They should also make sure that tables are arranged appropriately, surfaces are immaculate, and the ambiance is inviting.

DIFFICULTIES WITH REGULATION AND COMPLIANCE

1. Licensure and Permissions

Difficulty: Getting past the convoluted network of regional, national, and local rules may be tough. The criteria for zoning restrictions, business licenses, and health permits may differ based on the location.

Solution: Learn about the special demands of each area you intend to operate. Compile an inventory of the licenses and permissions that are necessary. To ensure perfect compliance, build relationships with area regulatory agencies and consider appointing a legal expert.

2. Guidelines for Health and Safety

Difficulty: Any food firm must operate in line with health and safety laws. Shutdowns or fines may follow noncompliance.

Resolved: Provide your personnel with rigorous health and safety training. Continually examine and enhance your practices for food safety. To comply with health requirements, invest money in high-quality equipment and conduct regular maintenance.

CHALLENGES IN OPERATIONS

Space Restraints:

Difficulty: A food truck's restricted interior may make it tough to produce and store food, which impacts production and service speed.

Fix: Make the most effective use of the space on your vehicle. To make the most of available space, organize your supplies and utilize equipment that saves room. Organize staff duties so they may move around and complete their responsibilities without being impeded.

Inventory Control

Difficulty: To minimize spoilage and shortages, inventory management in a limited space demands thorough planning.

Remedy: To monitor supply levels and expiration dates, put in place an inventory management system. Establish a regular ordering schedule and establish ties with reputable suppliers. Reduce your dependency on long-term storage by choosing seasonal, fresh foods.

The Reliability of Equipment

Difficulty: Equipment failure may create large losses and interrupt operations.

Remedy: Purchase strong, quality equipment meant for food truck usage. Maintain your equipment regularly and plan for unforeseen repairs. Maintain an inventory of critical spare parts and create relationships with neighbouring repair providers.

Monetary Troubles

1. Finances and Cash Movement

Difficulty: It may be challenging to manage cash flow and secure initial funding, especially in the early years of a business.

Remedy: Write a clear business plan explaining your projected growth and financial needs. Investigate additional sources of money, including investors, grants, crowdsourcing, and small business loans. Strictly manage your finances by making a budget, keeping track of your expenditures, and storing up money for emergencies.

2. Variations Seasonal

Difficulty: There may be considerable seasonal changes in food truck sales in terms of both revenue and customer traffic.

Solution: Sell things, cater gatherings and festivals, and grow your revenue sources by taking part in these activities. Create a marketing campaign that emphasizes your brand during off-peak periods by presenting seasonal menu items or unique discounts.

ISSUES WITH COMPETITION AND MARKETING

1. Establishing a clients

Difficulty: It may be tough to pull in and maintain customers in a competitive sector.

Solution: The key is to develop a unique brand identity that sets your food truck apart from the competitors. Develop a committed customer by employing internet marketing and social media. Involve your consumers by offering them something of a memorable eating experience, listening to their opinions, and establishing loyalty programs.

2. Position and Movement

Difficulty: Securing exceptional locations, especially in popular regions, may be challenging and competitive.

Solution: To locate profitable sites, extensively evaluate the market. Create an adaptive itinerary that will help you alter sites in response to patterns in customer traffic. Inform customers of your whereabouts using location-based apps and social media.

CHALLENGES WITH STAFFING

1. STAFF HIRING AND RETENTION

Difficulty: It could be challenging to locate trustworthy individuals with the requisite abilities who can function in a fast-paced, mobile environment.

Recommendation: To lure in top people, give excellent remuneration and bonuses. Establish growth and development prospects in a suitable work environment. Establish extensive training programs to ensure personnel are equipped for the special challenges of managing a food truck.

2. Staff Attrition

Difficulty: Excessive turnover rates could pose challenges for operations and impair the quality of services.

Solution: The solution is to establish a welcoming and exciting work atmosphere. Give workers clear prospects for professional advancement and recognize and reward their successes. Interview departing staff to find out why they're leaving and to address any lingering problems.

CHALLENGES WITH TECHNOLOGY

1. POS (Point of Sale) Systems

Challenge: It may be tough to set up and maintain a productive point-of-sale system that performs efficiently in a mobile situation.

Fix: Get a POS system that is trustworthy, compatible with mobile devices, and can be connected with other corporate operations such as inventory control and customer relationship management (CRM). Make sure the crew gets adequate training to guarantee the simplicity of use of your point-of-sale system.

2. Internet Presence:

Difficulty: It takes time and expertise to establish an intriguing and vibrant online presence.

Solution: Create a robust digital marketing strategy with regular email newsletters, user-friendly websites, and social media updates. If budgets permit, take into consideration employing a digital marketing specialist or business to supervise your online presence.

DIFFICULTIES IN CUSTOMER SERVICE

1. Expectations from Customers:

Difficulty: In a frenetic, mobile atmosphere, fulfilling and exceeding customer expectations may be tough.

Solution: Emphasize friendliness, efficiency, and problem-solving in your training programs for staff members to give great customer service. To uncover areas that require growth, acquire and assess customer feedback regularly. To enhance the customer experience, create reward programs and special promotions.

2. Resolving Grievances:

Challenge: Retaining a good reputation depends upon reacting effectively to customer complaints.

Resolution: Establish a well-defined method for addressing complaints, comprising of carefully hearing the customer out, swiftly listening to their difficulties, and ensuring that the consumer is happy. Make the most of consumer complaints to strengthen your services and avoid future instances of the same issues.

INNOVATION AND FLEXIBILITY
1. Staying Current with Trends:

Challenge: Research and innovation must be continual to remain current on culinary trends and customer preferences.

Recommendations: Update your menu regularly to take into consideration the newest culinary trends and client preferences. Keep up with the newest trends by engaging in food truck communities and attending industry events. Try out new recipes and concepts, and gather feedback from consumers to better what you're giving.

2. Getting Used to Shifting Markets

The food truck sector confronts a changing environment owing to the introduction of new companies and increasing customer demands.

o Solution: Continue to be adaptable and flexible by keeping an eye on customer attitudes and market trends. Always be ready to change your business strategy in reaction to market developments. Encourage new thoughts and techniques by fostering an inventive culture within your organization.

CHAPTER 7: EXPANDING AND DEVELOPING

GROWING YOUR ENTERTAINMENT

Scaling a food truck or restaurant company includes progressively increasing operations to satisfy increased demand, enhance income, and expand into new regions while maintaining standards of quality, consistency, and profitability. To achieve long-term success in the competitive food service market, companies must carefully plan and follow out their development strategy, whether they are growing from a single food truck to several locations or converting a restaurant concept into a franchise.

Establishing a food truck or restaurant company could require geographical development via the addition of additional sites. To fulfill demand and increase the user base, this may entail executing the same concept in other neighborhoods, cities, or locations. However, in order to select ideal places with significant demand and development potential, expansion needs full market research, including demographic study, competitive evaluation, and feasibility studies. To ensure successful expansion and seamless operations across numerous locations, organizations must also address problems including site selection, lease negotiations, regulatory and licensing requirements, staff and training needs.

Another common approach to establish a food truck or restaurant company is by franchising, which allows business owners to reproduce the concept, brand, and operations in conjunction with franchisees who fund and operate individual sites. Due to the fact that franchisees bear the costs associated with establishing and managing additional locations while gaining access to established procedures, ongoing support from the franchisor, and existing brand awareness, franchising offers businesses a scalable expansion strategy with low capital investment and operational risks. To assure consistency and quality across franchise locations and protect the integrity of the brand, franchising demands the preparation of detailed franchise agreements, operating manuals, training courses, and support systems.

Organizations may extend their operations by increasing their product or service offerings and diversifying their income sources, in addition to expanding geographically and via franchising. Offering additional menu items, catering services, food delivery alternatives, retail sales, or private event hosting are some methods to react to changing customer tastes and market trends while making more cash. Through diversification, firms may take advantage of new possibilities and promote development without having to spend much in new equipment or extend their operations by making the most of their current infrastructure, customer base, and brand value.

Another method to establish a food truck or restaurant is to invest in automation and technology, which helps companies to enhance production, improve customer happiness, and streamline operations. To enhance operations, decrease labor costs, and boost throughput, this may involve putting in place point-of-sale systems, online ordering platforms, inventory management software, kitchen automation tools, and delivery logistics solutions. Organizations can manage higher quantities, expand more efficiently, and maintain quality and consistency all at the same time by employing technology.

Furthermore, by increasing their reach, getting access to new markets, and merging resources, judicious partnerships and collaborations with other companies or organizations may benefit in the expansion of food truck and restaurant operations. This could involve cross-promotional activities, co-branding projects, cooperative events or pop-ups, or supplier alliances to employ complimentary talents and competencies and build win-win connections that support growth and improve brand recognition.

EXTENSION AND PROMOTIONS

A sensible approach employed by food truck and restaurant enterprises to generate income streams, meet a broad variety of consumer tastes, and adapt to altering market trends is providing diversity. Businesses may broaden their consumer base, boost sales prospects, and lessen the hazards inherent with depending just on one product or service by diversifying their menu options, income streams, and services. Diversification helps food truck and restaurant enterprises to stay competitive and adaptable in the constantly changing food service market, whether by menu development, the introduction of fresh culinary ideas, catering services, or the investigation of additional income sources.

Expanding the menu offerings to meet a greater variety of dietary requirements, tastes, and culinary possibilities is one strategy to achieve diversity and attract a bigger client base. This may involve altering up the menu to satisfy a variety of dietary demands and preferences, such as vegetarian, vegan, gluten-free, or allergy-friendly alternatives, or adding new dishes or seasonal specials. Businesses may attract in clients with a range of tastes and boost the chance of repeat business and word-of-mouth referrals by having a diverse menu.

Businesses may extend their menus and provide new services by introducing fusion cuisines or innovative culinary ideas that take advantage of rising trends in food and culture. To make meals distinctive and memorable, this may involve adding tastes from foreign nations, making recipes inspired by street food, or coming up with innovative variations on established dishes. Organizing themed events, like sushi pop-ups, taco nights, or barbecue festivals, could enhance foot traffic and sales prospects by drawing new consumers and building enthusiasm about the brand. In addition, product diversification may entail branching out into new service categories like meal kits, food delivery, or catering in order to accommodate the changing demands and tastes of clients. By offering catering services for corporate events, private parties, or special occasions, companies may increase their income streams and leverage their culinary experience and reputation to accommodate bigger groups and parties. Similar to this, selling meal kit or food delivery services helps companies to engage clients outside of their physical presence, take advantage of the rising desire for flexibility and convenience, and build their clientele.

Another method food truck and restaurant enterprises may develop and generate more money is to look into other revenue sources like retail sales, branded items, or culinary lessons. Offering branded items to consumers, including t-shirts, caps, or tote bags with the company's logo or philosophy, may create extra income streams and boost customer loyalty. Businesses may exploit customer desire for luxury ingredients and culinary experiences by supplying branded items like sauces, spices, or packaged goods. This helps firms enhance their brand presence beyond the eating experience. Furthermore, giving cooking courses, seminars, or culinary events helps companies to engage with clients, exhibit their culinary skills, generate extra cash, and enhance the entire client experience.

PARTNERSHIP OPPORTUNITIES

For food truck and restaurant companies wishing to enhance their brand recognition, expand into new regions, and leverage on the entrepreneurial energy of their franchisees, franchising provides an enticing choice. Companies may leverage the funds, assets, and local expertise of franchisees to build additional sites by franchising their brand. This enables them to take benefit of the existing brand awareness, operating processes, and support network supplied by the franchisor. A scalable development approach that lets firms expand fast and economically while dispersing risk and sharing rewards with franchise partners is franchising.

A main advantage of franchising for food truck and restaurant operations is its ability to swiftly grow and earn market dominance. Companies may grow quicker and more cheaply into new areas by collaborating with franchisees who are ready to invest in and operate individual units. This is in contrast to conventional techniques of growth. Franchisees allow firms to operate several sites concurrently and take advantage of demand in a range of geographic regions by offering their local market knowledge, skills, and financial resources.

In compared to company-owned growth, franchising gives organizations a scalable expansion plan with reduced financial needs and operational dangers. Franchisees frequently pay franchise fees and royalties to the franchisor in return for taking on the costs of creating and managing new sites, including leasehold renovations, equipment purchases, recruiting personnel, and marketing expenditures. This makes it feasible for firms to grow their reach without having to pay major upfront fees or take on debt, freeing up resources for marketing, brand building, and other vital business operations.

brand and support long-term growth and profitability by choosing qualified and dedicated franchise partners who share their vision, values, and dedication to quality and customer service.

CHAPTER 8: UNDERSTANDING THE NEED FOR SCALING

To develop your food truck business and enhance profitability and market awareness, you must scale your operations. It's necessary to examine your existing business performance before going into the details. Are you frequently meeting your sales goals? Do you possess a committed clientele? Does your product have greater demand than you can satisfy right now? It may be time to consider about scaling if the replies are in the affirmative.

THE ART OF STRATEGIC PLANNING

1. Research on the market and feasibility study

Determine New Locations with Possible Demand for Your Offerings: Identify new markets by undertaking in-depth market research. Seek for sites that pull the individuals in your target demographic, such as crowded streets, festivals, and events.

Competition Analysis: Examine competitors in the freshly established markets. To discover your unique selling proposition (USP), examine their pros and downsides.

Customer feedback: Use customer input to enhance your services and menu. Recognize the qualities of your food truck that consumers find attractive and exploit those elements to pull in new customers at different places.

2.Budgeting

Budgeting: Create a complete financial plan that provides for the upfront expenditures of expansion, such as purchasing new cars, gear, licenses, and people. Include operating expenses such as ingredients, fuel, marketing, and maintenance.

Financing: Examine your prospects for obtaining money, including crowdsourcing, investors, and small business loans. Show potential investors your successful business plan, stressing your opportunity for expansion.

3.Model of Business

Franchising: If you operate a food truck business, consider about franchising. Because franchisees pay the bulk of the beginning expenditures, this model allows you to develop swiftly with minimum financial investment. Create a franchise model with spelled-out regulations and channels of assistance for franchise owners.

many Trucks: Managing numerous trucks directly under your command is an extra option. Although it demands a lot of money and time, this technique assures consistency and quality.

OPERATIONAL GROWTH

1.Place Strategy

Permanent positions: Obtain permanent positions in popular locales such as parks, commercial hubs, and college campuses. Establishing permanent venues could result in a committed customer and reliable cash streams.

Event Catering: Consider getting into this sector. To serve at festivals, corporate events, and private parties, cooperate with the local event planners. This enhances sales and improves brand awareness concurrently.

2. Menu Enhancement

Standardize Recipes: To assure consistency in every configuration, standardize your recipes. Educate your personnel effectively and give extensive recipe instructions.

Offer limited-time or seasonal meals to peak customers' attention and keep them coming back for more.

3. Employees and Education:

Hiring: Find competent and motivated people. Maintaining quality and customer service while expanding demands a good team.

Training Programs: Provide new people with extensive training. Make sure they are aware of your menu, standards of customer service, and corporate values.

4. Technological Coordination

Point of Sale (POS) Systems: Invest in state-of-the-art POS systems that manage inventory, track sales, streamline operations, and give extensive data.

Mobile Apps: Create a mobile application for online ordering, loyalty programs, and customer engagement. Apps may enhance recurring business and improve customer convenience.

PROMOTING AND DEVELOPING BRANDS

1. Brand Coherence

visual Identity: Ensure that the visual identity of all vehicles, marketing material, and digital platforms is consistent. Packaging, color schemes, and logos fit into this category.

Brand Voice: Create a unique voice for your brand that connects with customers and conveys your views. In all of your talks, utilize this voice consistently.

2. DIGITAL ADVERTISING

Social media: Use social media platforms to publicize your food truck. Distribute engaging stuff like customer reviews, behind-the-scenes images, and special promotions.

Search engine optimization and online presence: Make sure your website is mobile-friendly and search engine-friendly. To boost the visibility of your firm in local searches, declare it on Google My Business and other online directories.

Email marketing: Create an email list and send out updates, specials, and event announcements on a regular basis. Customized emails can promote sales and create customer loyalty.

3.Interaction with the Community

Local Partnerships: To improve your reach, collaborate with influencers and firms in your town. Events, collaborative marketing, and social media shoutouts may attract in new customers.

Charities and Sponsorships: Participate in local initiatives and offer financial assistance for area meetings. By doing this, you not only boost the impression of your brand but also win over new customers.

TAKING CARE OF GROWTH

1.Control of Quality

Regular Audits: Perform audits on a regular basis to make sure that health and safety rules are being followed. Check the cleanliness, food safety, and operational efficacy of vehicles.

Consumer input: Constantly gather and study consumer information to discover areas in need of growth.

2. Management of Finances

Cost Control: Pay great attention to your expenditures and explore for solutions to minimize money without losing quality. To boost productivity, negotiate better pricing with suppliers and streamline operations.

Utilize accounting software to track profits, losses, and other critical performance measures. Examine financial accounts regularly in order to make sensible selections.

3. Scalability

Flexible Operations: Verify the scalability of your operations. Having measures in place that can handle increased demand without losing service quality is one approach to achieve this.

Growth Strategy: Formulate a long-term strategy for growth that incorporates new revenue sources, product diversification, and prospective market expansions.

ASSESSMENT OF ACHIEVEMENT

1. Important Performance Measures (KPIs)

Revenue and Sales: Monitor revenue and sales growth at every location. To uncover areas for improvement and high-performing locations, compare performance.

Customer Retention: To ensure loyalty and satisfaction, measure and assess customer retention rates and customer feedback.

Operational Efficiency: Monitor data on order fulfillment delays, inventory turnover, and labor productivity to determine operational efficiency.

2. Ongoing Enhancement:

Feedback Loops: To consistently better your services and processes, build feedback loops with both staff and customers.

Innovation: Keep aware of changes in the sector. To remain ahead of the competition, continually present novel ideas and technologies.

CHAPTER 9: TECHNOLOGY AND INNOVATION

Technology and innovation are crucial for enhancing operational efficiency, raising customer happiness, and accelerating corporate progress in the constantly evolving food truck market. Taking advantage of the most current advances could provide your food truck business a competitive edge and long-term profitability. This in-depth booklet shows how innovation and technology are altering the food truck sector and how you can utilize these tools to your advantage.

POS (Point of Sale) Systems

Portable Point of Sale Systems

Innovation: Mobile point-of-sale (POS) technologies have totally transformed the way food trucks process payments. Since these systems are portable, transactions may be carried out anywhere.

Advantages: They offer speed, flexibility, and convenience, enabling food truck entrepreneurs to serve consumers rapidly and efficiently. In order to optimize procedures and give meaningful business data, mobile point-of-sale (POS) systems may also be coupled with inventory management and customer relationship management (CRM) software.

2. MAKING CONTACTLESS PAYMENTS:

Progress: More consumers are utilizing contactless payment solutions like mobile wallets and tap-to-pay.

Advantages: By delivering a speedy and secure way to pay, these payment options enhance the customer experience. Additionally, they decrease errors and theft by removing the requirement for touching cash.

MANAGEMENT OF INVENTORY

1. Automated Inventory Management:

Advancement: Real-time inventory level monitoring is made feasible by automated inventory management systems, which utilize software and sensors.

Advantages: These approaches assure that vital components are constantly available, cut down on waste, and eliminate overstocking. In order to discover trends and optimize stock levels, they also give data analytics.

2. Chain of Supply Integration

Progress: A seamless supply chain from suppliers to the food truck is achieved by integrating inventory management.

Advantages: This link minimizes expenditures and maintains appropriate inventory levels by automating ordering operations and provides real-time supply status information.

ORDERING AND DELIVERY ONLINE

1. Smartphone Apps and Web Pages

Advancement: With specialized smartphone apps and websites, a number of food trucks now enable online ordering.

Advantages: This technology cuts down on wait times and increases the customer experience by allowing customers to place orders ahead of time. It also provides food trucks the potential to reach more people and generate more money.

2. Services Provided by a Third Party

Development: It has risen in popularity to partner with outside delivery services like Grubhub, Door Dash, and Uber Eats.

Advantages: Customers who prefer home delivery may profit from these arrangements, which widen the customer base beyond the food truck's local territory. Through the distribution networks, they also give marketing and advertising options.

CLIENT RELATIONSHIP ADMINISTRATION (CRM)

1. Software for CRM

Advancement: Data and customer interactions are handled by food trucks with the help of CRM software.

Benefits include the capacity to monitor customer preferences, assess purchasing behavior, and deliver customized marketing. Building loyalty programs, boosting customer service, and tailoring marketing efforts are all achievable with this data.

2. Loyalty Initiatives

Advancement: CRM systems and digital loyalty programs may be integrated to reward loyal customers.

Benefits: By offering incentives for recurrent business, these programs enhance customer loyalty. Additionally, by supplying important information on customer habits and preferences, they may assist in the enhancement of marketing approaches.

SOCIAL MEDIA AND MARKETING

1. Social Media Site

Development: Social media platforms like Facebook, Twitter, and Instagram are useful outlets for food truck marketing.

Advantages: They give an economical tool to communicate with customers, reach a large audience, and develop a community. Updates, sales, behind-the-scenes films, and client endorsements may all be published on social media to boost brand visibility and customer participation.

2. Partnerships with Influencers

Development: Working with social media influencers may increase advertising strategies.

Benefits: Influencers may help the food truck get viewed by a bigger audience, make real recommendations, and drive traffic to the vehicle. Credibility and brand recognition may both be boosted by these partnerships.

INFORMATION ANALYTICS

1. Analysis of sales data

Advancement: By studying sales data, one may learn more about the most popular menu items, peak selling times, and customer demographics.

Advantages: By employing this data, personnel strategies, pricing systems, and menus may all be optimized. It also pinpoints regions in need of growth and prospects for expansion.

2. Analysis of client feedback

The technique of receiving and assessing customer opinion via surveys, reviews, and comments on social media is an innovation.

Advantages: This technique delivers valuable information on consumer satisfaction and possible development opportunities. It enhances the complete customer experience, helps detect trends, and takes immediate action to remedy issues.

SAFE FOOD HANDLING AND PREPARATION

1. Intelligent Kitchen Appliances

Advancement: The utilization of remotely controlled and viewable smart kitchen equipment.

Advantages: These appliances boost production by minimizing the potential of human error, maintaining regularity, and automating cooking activities. They also maintain proper temperature controls and inform operators of any concerns, which promotes food safety.

2. Monitoring Food Safety

Advancement: Real-time temperature, humidity, and other important element tracking is made feasible by digital food safety monitoring systems.

Advantages: By assuring conformity to health rules, these systems limit the chance of foodborne diseases. Data logs that are important for audits and inspections are also given by them.

EFFICIENCY IN OPERATIONS

1. Route Optimization Program

Development: Software for route optimization aids in developing the best potential routes for food trucks.

Advantages: By cutting down on travel time and fuel expenditures, this technology assures fast arrivals in congested regions. It also boosts the ability to serve more customers and generate income.

2. Instruments for Staff Scheduling

Progress: The scheduling technique is automated by digital staff scheduling technology.

Advantages: These solutions ensure the proper quantity of personnel based on peak hours and sales estimates. By offering workers clear and consistent timetables, they can minimize scheduling hassles and boost employee happiness.

Eco-Friendly and Sustainable Methodologies

1. Environmentally Sustainable Packaging

Innovation: Using packaging materials that are compostable and biodegradable.

Advantages: By employing these materials, the food truck sector has a less negative environmental impact. They are appealing to customers who care about the environment and may give a major competitive advantage.

2. Energy-Consumptive Equipment

Advancement: Purchasing appliances and utensils that consume less energy.

Advantages: This equipment minimizes operating expenditures and energy utilization. In addition, it helps meet sustainability targets and enhances the company's overall profitability.

Creative Menu and Service Concepts

1. Novel Menu Items:

Innovation: Adding fresh, in-vogue, and seasonal foods to the menu on a regular basis.

Advantages: By keeping the menu fresh, this method brings in repeat business. Additionally, it offers an edge over rivals by allowing the testing of fresh hypotheses and concepts.

2. Adjustable Purchases

Innovation: Providing digital ordering systems with customized food selections.

Advantages: By addressing unique dietary demands and preferences, this flexibility enhances the customer experience. By giving additional customizing possibilities, it may also enhance sales.

CONCLUSION

SUMMARY KEY POINTS

In conclusion, there are numerous prospects for success in the food truck and restaurant businesses for entrepreneurs. However, conquering the obstacles of this competitive market needs meticulous planning, savvy decision-making, and an attention on essential operating areas. Below is a synopsis of the key themes addressed in this thorough overview:

1. OVERVIEW OF THE FOOD BUSINESS

Success in the food industry relies on having a thorough awareness of the company's dynamics, including client preferences, market trends, and the degree of competition. Completing extensive market research, establishing target demographics, and building a unique value proposition that separates the firm from competition are key.

2. The benefits of food trucks and restaurants

These are various and include things like flexibility, mobility, reduced startup expenses for food trucks, higher earning potential, bigger seating capacity, and a broader assortment of menu items for restaurants.

3. business registration and licensing

Establishing a legitimate and compliant operation needs a number of key processes, including registering the firm, getting permits, licenses, and certifications, and adhering to health and safety standards. It's necessary to research and comprehend the relevant rules and norms regulating food operations within the local government.

4. Health and Safety Regulations

In order to safeguard customers' health and well-being and to comply with regulatory requirements, it is vital to maintain high standards of food safety, cleanliness, and hygiene. Strong food safety regulations, personnel training, and periodic inspections are vital for ensuring adherence and maintaining customer trust.

5. Permissions and Inspection: Obtaining

permissions and going through inspections by regulatory agencies and health authorities are key stages in beginning a food truck or restaurant company. For companies to remain in compliance and keep out of trouble, they need to make sure they have the right approvals and go through frequent inspections.

6. Selecting a Location

A food truck or restaurant business's potential to prosper is heavily determined by its location. When picking a location for the company, variables like foot traffic, visibility, accessibility, competitiveness, demographics, and zoning restrictions should be carefully taken into consideration.

7. Equipment and Supplies

Investing in top-notch kitchen equipment, utensils, and supplies is crucial to keeping things going smoothly and offering customers with great food and service. When selecting equipment, organizations should look about energy efficiency, durability, and usefulness.

They should also barter with suppliers to acquire good rates.

8. Menu Development

Gaining and maintaining clients relies on establishing a complete and attractive menu that appeals to target consumers and showcases the distinctive traits and preferences of the company. To stay competitive, companies should perform market research, look into client preferences and dietary trends, and update and refresh their menu options on a regular basis.

9. Budgeting and Identity

For financial stability and brand distinctiveness, setting a detailed budget, properly controlling expenses, and building a strong brand identity are crucial. To establish a committed client base and enjoy sustainable success, companies should put a high focus on budgeting, keep expenditures under control, and make investments in branding, marketing, and customer experience efforts.

10. Staffing and Training

Providing exceptional customer service and attaining operational success rely on identifying and employing skilled people, providing them with proper training, and promoting a pleasant work environment. To retain a healthy and effective work environment, firms should encourage employee development, respect and reward success, and foster cooperation and communication.

11. Inventory management

Reducing expenditures, reducing waste, and ensuring product availability all rely on good inventory management. To enhance profitability and please consumers, firms should build inventory monitoring systems, optimize inventory levels, and adhere to best practices for rotating, storing, and restocking items.

12. Customer service

Gaining new business, promoting repeat business, and establishing brand loyalty all rely on giving top-notch customer service. To create amazing dining experiences, companies should emphasize providing visitors a warm greeting, taking and carrying out orders precisely, communicating effectively, and anticipating and going above and beyond what consumers need and expect.

13. Diversification and options

Food truck and restaurant enterprises may better adapt to shifting market trends, attract in new consumers, and enhance sales potential by diversifying their menu options, services, and revenue streams. To expand their offers and encourage growth, organizations can think about prospects for menu design, catering, retail sales, and technological integration.

14. Opportunities for Franchising

Franchising provides a tempting opportunity for firms wishing to increase their market reach, boost their brand recognition, and harness the innovative spirit of their franchisees. Organizations may hasten their growth, successfully expand their operations, and build a network of wealthy franchise locations that support long-term profitability by cooperating with dedicated franchisees.

FUTURE PLAN

Future expectations for food trucks and restaurants are exciting and dynamic, driven by shifting market conditions, technological improvements, and expanding client demand. The industry provides significant chances for innovation, expansion, and trend adaption, especially in the face of obstacles like greater competition, expanding costs, and altering client preferences. The forecast for food trucks and restaurants is as follows:

1. *Integration of Technology:* The future of food trucks and restaurants will be strongly affected by technology in the years to come. Technological improvements in kitchen automation, delivery logistics, and smartphone ordering and payment systems are totally transforming how companies function and connect with their audience. Organizations may enhance customer happiness, boost productivity, and accelerate processes by adopting technology into their everyday operations.

2. *Digital Transformation:* Due to shifting client preferences and habits, it is projected that the trend toward digital channels and online ordering will gain up pace in the future years. Food trucks and restaurants will rely more and more on social media, internet, and smartphone apps to sell their food, engage with guests, and accelerate transactions. In a world where competition is rising, implementing digital transformation helps organizations to extend their reach, boost their exposure, and increase revenues.

3. Emphasis on Sustainability and Health: Customers are seeking for more sustainable and healthier food options as a consequence of rising knowledge of environmental and health problems. In response, food trucks and cafes will give a bigger assortment of locally produced, organic, and plant-based cuisine in addition to eco-friendly packaging and waste reduction practices. In addition to addressing consumer demand, an emphasis on sustainability and health is aligned with ideals of environmental stewardship and social responsibility.

4. personalization and *customization*: As consumers demand for unique and personalized dining experiences, personalization and customization will play a greater part in food service in the future. Changeable menu selections, interactive dining experiences, and personalized recommendations based on customer tastes and dietary constraints will all be accessible at food trucks and restaurants. Businesses may boost customer pleasure, develop customer loyalty, and stand out in a competitive market by delivering exceptional experiences.

5. Ghost Kitchens and Virtual Brands: The advent of these ideas has provided food truck and restaurant enterprises new options to increase their client bases and market share. Ghost kitchens, commonly referred to as dark kitchens or virtual kitchens, are commercial kitchens that are exclusively utilized to cook meals for takeout and delivery. This allows firms to fulfill orders without needing to maintain physical stores. Virtual brands are restaurant concepts that operate entirely online, employing the culinary infrastructure already in place to develop unique menu items and attract in new consumers. Using virtual brands and ghost kitchens helps companies to test new ideas, establish new revenue streams, and adapt to changing consumer expectations in the digital arena.

6. Community engagement and Social Responsibility: The survival of food truck and restaurant operations in the future will rely on community engagement and social responsibility.

Companies will actively engage in community events, promote neighborhood initiatives, and interact with customers via social media and other channels. Strong community links and a dedication to social responsibility may help firms acquire the respect, loyalty, and trust of stakeholders, including customers and workers.

7. *Adaptability and Resilience:* In order for food truck and restaurant enterprises to succeed in the future, they will need to be able to adjust to evolving customer preferences and market situations. In the face of evolving market trends, regulatory restrictions, and economic downturns, companies need to be adaptable, inventive, and resilient. Organizations may position themselves for long-term success and sustainability in the fast-paced food service market by staying ahead of trends, anticipating customer wants, and consistently enhancing their services and processes.

www.ingramcontent.com/pod-product-compliance
Lightning Source LLC
Chambersburg PA
CBHW071516220526
45472CB00003B/1043